롤러코스터
이래서 강력추천합니다!

체계적인 학습 | 초등학교 교육 과정을 충실히 반영하고 교과서 지문을 최대한 활용함으로써 학생들이 배워야 할 주요 학습 내용을 체계적으로 익힐 수 있도록 하였습니다.

학년별 맞춤 학습 | 모든 학년에서 표현과 낱말 학습을 기본으로 하되, 1·2학년은 Phonics, 3·4학년은 Reading & Writing, 5·6학년은 Grammar를 다루는 등, 각 학년별 주요 학습 영역을 중점적으로 다룸으로써 학년별 맞춤 학습을 추구하였습니다.

균형적인 학습 | 읽기, 쓰기 학습뿐만 아니라 오디오 CD와 동영상 CD를 활용한 듣기, 말하기 학습을 통해 영어의 4개 영역(Listening, Speaking, Reading, Writing)을 고루 마스터할 수 있도록 하였습니다.

자발적인 학습 | Song, Chant를 통해 표현을 자연스럽게 익히고, Cartoon을 통해 배운 내용을 재미있게 정리하는 등 다양한 Activity를 통해 학생들이 흥미를 가지고 적극적으로 수업에 참여할 수 있도록 하였습니다.

동영상을 통한 원어민과의 학습 | 원어민의 발음과 입모양을 동영상 CD를 통해 정확히 인지하고 학습자의 발음을 녹음해 원어민의 발음과 비교하여 들어 보게 함으로써 학습자 스스로 발음을 교정할 수 있는 기회를 제공하였습니다.

set 구성

01 Student Book_ Unit 1, 3

Conversation

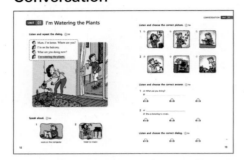

초등영어 교과과정과 연계된 표현을 학습하고,
다양한 활동을 통해 표현을 익혀 봐요.

Words

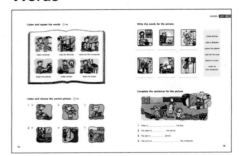

생활 영어 표현과 관련된 낱말을 학습하고,
재미있게 낱말을 익혀 봐요.

Reading

표현에 대한 이해력을 높이고, 각종 경시대회 및
TOEFL iBT에 대비할 수 있는 문제를 풀어 봐요.

Writing

학습한 표현을 써 보면서, 자유롭게 활용할 수
있는 능력을 키워 봐요.

Cartoon

재미있는 만화를 통해 이미 학습한 표현과
낱말을 종합 정리해 봐요.

Test

테스트를 통해 학습한 표현 및 낱말에 대한
학습 성취도를 점검해 봐요.

Student Book_ Unit 2, 4

Cartoon

재미있는 만화를 통해 앞으로 배울 핵심 문법
사항을 미리 알아봐요.

Grammar point 1

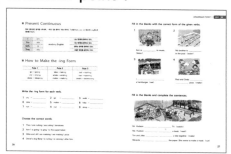

핵심 문법 사항을 익히고 다양한 활동을 통해
응용해 봐요.

Grammar point 2

핵심 문법 사항을 익히고 다양한 활동을 통해
응용해 봐요.

Story

학습한 문법을 활용한 흥미로운 이야기를 읽고
문제를 풀어 봐요.

Story words

이야기에서 학습한 낱말을 예문을 통해
종합 정리해 봐요.

Test

테스트를 통해 학습한 문법에 대한 이해도와
응용력을 평가해 봐요.

02 Workbook

낱말을 따라 쓴 다음, 우리말에 해당하는
낱말을 직접 써 봐요.

표현을 따라 쓴 다음, 우리말에 해당하는
표현을 직접 써 봐요.

잘 듣고, 빈칸에 알맞은 낱말과
표현을 자신있게 써 봐요.

03 권말 테스트

낱말 및 표현에 관한 문제를 풀면서 그동안 쌓은
실력을 마음껏 발휘해 봐요.
(Achievement Test / Final Test)

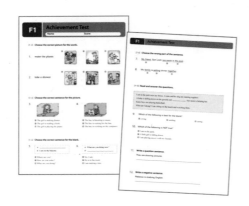

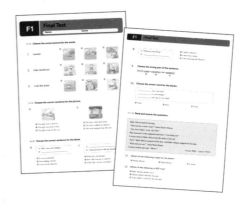

04 동영상 CD

Conversation

초등영어 교과과정과 연계된 표현을 배워 봐요.

Words

생활영어 표현과 관련된 낱말을 배워 봐요.

Speak

학습한 낱말들을 녹음해 원어민의 발음과
비교해 봐요.

05 오디오 CD

Student Book, Workbook의 내용과 노래 및
챈트가 담겨 있어요.

Learning Points

F1

Unit Title	Theme	Function (Unit 1&3) Grammar (Unit 2&4)	Conversation (Unit 1&3) Language Item (Unit 2&4)
1 I'm Watering the Plants	Present Continuous	· Talking about what one is doing	Mom, I'm home. Where are you? I'm on the balcony. What are you doing now? I'm watering the plants.
2 What Is Alice Doing?	Present Continuous	· Present continuous: how to make -ing form, making question, negative sentences	I am going to school. She is not playing the piano. Are they drawing pictures?
3 How Was Your Vacation?	Past Simple	· Expressing experiences of past using past simple	How was your vacation? It was great. I had a great time. What did you do during your vacation? I took a trip to Hawaii with my family.
4 I Went to the Cinema	How / What Past Simple	· Question words: how / what · Past simple of verbs: Regular and irregular verbs	How did you get to the library? What did you do in London? Jenny visited her cousin yesterday. I swam in the sea with my brother.

F2

Unit Title	Theme	Function (Unit 1&3) Grammar (Unit 2&4)	Conversation (Unit 1&3) Language Item (Unit 2&4)
1 I Have a Cold	Sickness Cause & Result	· Expressing one's sickness	Are you OK? You look sick. I have a cold. Why are you so busy? Because I have to finish this work.
2 Why Is the Alien in Our Garden?	Cause & Result	· Question 'why' · Conjunction 'because'	Why are you so happy? Because I got a present. I don't eat pizza because I'm on a diet.
3 Would You Like to Come?	Suggestion	· Suggestion	Would you like to come to my house? Yes, I'd love to. Come to my house by 5 o'clock. Okay. See you then.
4 Would You Help Me, Please?	Would	· would like to · Modal verb 'would'	Would you help me, please? Would you like to try this pie? I would like to look at the menu.

F3

Unit Title	Theme	Function (Unit 1&3) Grammar (Unit 2&4)	Conversation (Unit 1&3) Language Item (Unit 2&4)
1 Turn Off the TV	Commands	· Imperatives: Positive / Negative	Turn off the TV. Don't watch TV.
2 Don't Take Photographs	Phrasal Verbs	· Imperatives · Phrasal verbs	Be careful. The picture fell down. Pick up the key.
3 I'm Going to Visit My Grandparents	Future Tense with 'be going to'	· Describing what someone is going to do	I'm going to visit my uncle tomorrow. Are you going to see a movie tomorrow?
4 What Are You Going to Eat?	Future Tense with 'be going to'	· Future tense with 'be going to': Yes / No questions / Wh-questions	What are you going to do this weekend? I'm going to stay home.

F4

Unit Title	Theme	Function (Unit 1 & 3) / Grammar (Unit 2 & 4)	Conversation (Unit 1 & 3) / Language Item (Unit 2 & 4)
❶ He Is Taller Than Your Father	Comparatives	· Comparing people, animals and things	He is taller than your father. The train is faster than the car. The gorilla is stronger than the monkey.
❷ He Is Faster Than Us	Comparatives	· The comparative	The bear is heavier than the monkey. The red car is better than the green car. The pizza is more delicious than the spaghetti.
❸ Sam Is the Tallest in My Class	Superlatives	· Expressing the superlative	Are you the tallest in your class? No, I'm not. Sam is the tallest in my class.
❹ Who Is the Most Beautiful in Town?	Superlatives	· The superlative	Joseph is the thinnest. Daniel's bike is the worst. This movie is the most interesting.

F5

Unit Title	Theme	Function (Unit 1 & 3) / Grammar (Unit 2 & 4)	Conversation (Unit 1 & 3) / Language Item (Unit 2 & 4)
❶ How Often Do You Visit the Museum?	Frequency Adverbs	· Explaining frequency	What do you usually do on weekends? I usually visit the museum with my family. How often do you get a haircut? I get a haircut three times a year.
❷ What I Always Bring Is	Frequency Adverbs	· Frequency adverbs	How often do you practice the piano? I practice the piano twice a week. I am always late for school. They rarely go abroad.
❸ Whose Bag Is This?	Possessions	· Talking about possessions	Whose bag is this? It's my bag. It's mine.
❹ It's Mine	Possessions	· Possessive adjectives and possessive pronouns	Whose toys are these? They are his. Whose hamsters are these? They are Tina's.

F6

Unit Title	Theme	Function (Unit 1 & 3) Grammar (Unit 2 & 4)	Conversation (Unit 1 & 3) Language Item (Unit 2 & 4)
1 How Do You Get to the Stadium?	Transportation	· Expressing ways of transportation and time	How do you get to the stadium? I get to the stadium by bus. How long does it take to the aquarium? It takes about 30 minutes.
2 How Long Do We Have to Wait?	How	· Question word 'how'	How is the weather? How do you feel? How many pencils do you have? How much sugar do you need?
3 Which Do You Want, Muffins or Doughnuts?	Preference	· Talking about one's preference	Which do you want, muffins or doughnuts? I want muffins, please.
4 Which Person Is His Mother, You or Her?	Conjunction 'or'	· Question word 'which' · Conjunction 'or'	Which color do you want, red or blue? I want blue. I will go camping in July or August. Do you want to watch TV or play outside?

Roller Coaster

Contents

UNIT 01 I'm Watering the Plants

Listen and repeat the dialog. T02

Mom, I'm home. Where are you?

I'm on the balcony.

What are you doing now?

I'm watering the plants.

Speak aloud. T03

1
work on the computer

2

listen to music

Listen and choose the correct picture. T04

1 ⓐ 　ⓑ 　ⓒ

2 ⓐ 　ⓑ 　ⓒ

Listen and choose the correct answer. T04

1 *A:* What are you doing?

　B: _____

2 *A:* _____

　B: She is listening to music.

Listen and choose the correct dialog. T04

Listen and repeat the words. T05

take a shower

wait for the bus

work on the computer

water the plants

make dinner

listen to music

Listen and choose the correct picture. T06

1 ⓐ  ⓑ  ⓒ

2 ⓐ  ⓑ  ⓒ

Write the words for the picture.

_____ _____ _____

_____ _____ _____

make dinner

take a shower

water the plants

wait for the bus

listen to music

work on
the computer

Complete the sentences for the picture.

Mike

1 Mike is _____ _____ the bus.

2 His sister is _____ the plants.

3 His dad is _____ dinner.

4 His mom is _____ _____ the computer.

Choose the correct sentence for the picture.

1

ⓐ The boy is watering the plants.

ⓑ The boy is drinking water.

ⓒ The boy is wearing a cap.

2

ⓐ The girl is making dinner.

ⓑ The girl is working on the computer.

ⓒ The girl is going to the park.

3

ⓐ The girl is reading a book.

ⓑ The girl is walking on the street.

ⓒ The girl is waiting for the bus.

4

ⓐ The boy is taking a shower.

ⓑ The boy is playing the piano.

ⓒ The boy is listening to music.

Match pairs to make dialogs.

 What are you doing?

 I'm on the balcony.

 Where are you?

 I'm making a kite.

 CHALLENGE!

Choose the correct sentence for the blank.

1 *A:* Mom, I'm home.

_____

B: I am on the balcony.

ⓐ What is it?

ⓑ Where are you?

ⓒ When do you come?

2 *A:* What is Mac doing?

B: _____

ⓐ He is 180cm tall.

ⓑ He is listening to music.

ⓒ He likes soccer very much.

Fill in the blanks to complete the summary.

Julie: Hi.

Kelly: Hi, Julie. What are you doing?

Julie: I'm making a cake.

Will you help me?

Kelly: Sure. It looks fun.

Let's make a delicious cake.

Julie is making a _____ and Kelly will _____ Julie.

Choose and write the sentence for the picture.

> A girl is reading a book.   A woman is making dinner.
>
> A boy is taking a shower.   A man is watering the plants.

_____

_____

_____

_____

Write the correct answer for the picture.

1

A: What is she doing?

B: _____

2

A: What is the girl doing?

B: _____

Unscramble and write the sentence.

1 reading   is   my brother   .   book   a

_____

2 doing   ?   what   is   Ann   now

_____

3 balcony   is   my father   on   the   .

_____

4 watering   .   Mr. Baker   is   flowers   the

_____

Complete the sentences for the picture.

My family had dinner and now we are having a rest.

My mother is _____ a book and my father is _____ the plants.

My sister is _____ to music.

Me? I am writing about my family.

Making a Kite??

Complete the cartoon. If necessary, change the form.

read (×2)

water the plants

make (×2)

What are you doing?

[1~4] Listen and number the pictures. 🔘 T07

[5~6] Listen and choose the correct picture. 🔘 T07

5   ⓐ    ⓑ    ⓒ

6   ⓐ    ⓑ    ⓒ

[7~8] Choose the correct word for the blank.

7 _____ is Sue doing now?

    ⓐ Who   ⓑ When   ⓒ What

8 Tom _____ on the computer in his room.

    ⓐ is playing   ⓑ is working   ⓒ is washing

[9~10] Choose the correct sentence for the blank.

9

> *A:* Judy, I am making dinner. Help me, please.
> *B:* OK, mom, but wait a moment.
> *A:* Why? What are you doing now?
> *B:* _____

    ⓐ I like salad.

    ⓑ I am hungry.

    ⓒ I am taking a shower.

10

> *Sam:* Good afternoon, Ms. Wilson.
> *Ms. Wilson:* Good afternoon, Sam.
> *Sam:* I want to meet Tony. Is he at home?
> *Ms. Wilson:* He is not at home now.
> *Sam:* _____
> *Ms. Wilson:* He is in the library.

    ⓐ How is he?   ⓑ Where is he?   ⓒ Where does he live?

Quiz

Q: It is 4 o'clock. What is Alice doing now?

A: She is _____ now.

Quiz

Q: Why is Alice crying?

A: Because of Ted's _____ .

■ Present Continuous

현재 진행 중인 동작을 나타내며, '~하고 있는 중이다'라는 뜻이다. 「be동사(am, are, is)+동사의 -ing형」의 형태를 지닌다.

I	am		나는 영어를 공부하고 있다.
You	are		너는 영어를 공부하고 있다.
Sally	is	studying English.	샐리는 영어를 공부하고 있다.
They	are		그들은 영어를 공부하고 있다.

■ How to Make the -ing Form

Rule 1	Rule 2	Rule 3
go → going cry → crying sleep → sleeping	take → taking smile → smiling make → making	cut → cutting run → running swim → swimming

Write the -ing form for each verb.

1 cry → _____   2 go → _____   3 walk → _____

6 take → _____   5 make → _____   6 hike → _____

7 run → _____   4 cut → _____   9 shop → _____

Choose the correct words.

1 They (are cutting / are cuting) tomatoes.

2 Ann (is going / is ging) to the supermarket.

3 Mike and Jill (are makeing / are making) pizza.

4 David's dog Benji (is runing / is running) after him.

Fill in the blanks with the correct form of the given verbs.

1

Ann is _____ to music.
(listen)

2

My brother is _____
in the pool. (swim)

3

I _____ _____
a hamburger. (eat)

4

Paul and Cindy _____
_____ pizza. (make)

Fill in the blanks and complete the sentences.

Mr. Hudson _____ _____ TV. (watch)

Ms. Hudson _____ _____ a book. (read)

Tim and Jake _____ _____ a kite together. (make)

Miranda _____ _____ the paper. She wants to make a mask. (cut)

■ Present Continuous: Question / Negative

Question	be동사를 주어 앞에 쓴다.
	The baby is crying. → Is the baby crying?
	She is watching TV. → Is she watching TV?
	You are doing your homework.
	→ Are you doing your homework?
Negative	not을 be동사 뒤에 쓴다.
	I am making pizza. → I am not making pizza.
	Amy is reading a book. → Amy is not reading a book.
	They are sleeping. → They are not sleeping.

Fill in the blanks for the picture.

1

A: _____ he playing the piano?

B: No, he is _____ playing the piano.
He is playing the violin.

2

A: _____ they eating spaghetti?

B: No, they are _____ eating spaghetti.
They are eating pizza.

Write a question sentence.

1 Tony is watching TV.

_____

2 You are going to school.

_____

3 They are eating hamburgers.

_____

Write a negative sentence.

1 I am doing my homework.

_____

2 My sister, Miranda is playing the piano.

_____

3 Mom and Dad are reading books.

_____

Unscramble and write the sentence.

1 | lunch | are | you | making | ? |

_____

2 | music | Mary | is | listening | to | not | . |

_____

Welcome to My School T08

I am Ting. I live in Beijing. Every morning
I walk to school with my sister Jiao.
Now I will show my school to you.

This is my school.
There are many students and we are good friends.
Look!
Some boys are playing soccer and some girls are
ⓐ run on the playground. I like soccer, too.

This is my classroom. My friends are drawing pictures and
my teacher, Ms. Lee is helping them. They are all smiling and look happy.

1 다음 중 Ting에 대한 설명으로 바르지 않은 것을 고르세요.

① 베이징에 살고 있다.

② 학교에 걸어서 간다.

③ 야구를 잘한다.

2 밑줄 친 ⓐ를 올바른 형태로 고쳐 쓰세요.

3 What are Ting's friends doing in the classroom?

①  ②  ③

This is a music room.

The students are singing and the teacher is playing the piano. They sound great.

This is a school library.

We have a lot of books and good computers here.

_____ ⓑ _____

and some students are working on the computers.

Now we are in a school _____ ⓒ _____.

We eat lunch here.

Some girls are eating sandwiches and

some boys are drinking milk.

The food is delicious.

Do you like my school? I love my school.

4 빈칸 ⓑ에 가장 어울리는 것을 고르세요.

① Many students are reading books

② Many students are watching TV

③ Many students are listening to music

5 빈칸 ⓒ에 알맞은 낱말을 고르세요.

① classroom   ② playground   ③ cafeteria

6 다음 중 윗글의 내용과 다른 그림을 고르세요.

①    ②    ③

Build up your word power.

⊙ **walk**

걷다: to go on foot

Every morning I _____ to school.

⊙ **sister**

언니, 여동생: a girl of the same parents as another

This is my _____ Jiao.

⊙ **student**

학생: someone who is studying at a school

My brother is a middle school _____.

⊙ **classroom**

교실: a room that you have lesson in a school

This is my _____.

⊙ **draw**

그리다: to make a picture with a pencil

My friends _____ a picture together.

⊙ **smile**

웃다, 미소짓다: to make a pleasant expression with the mouth

They _____.

32

⊙ **sing**

노래하다: to make music with voice

The students _____.

⊙ **library**

도서관: a room where books, records, videos, etc. are kept
for study, reading or lending

This is a school _____.

⊙ **cafeteria**

학교 식당: a self-service restaurant especially in a school

Now we are in a school _____.

⊙ **talk**

말하다: to express something by speaking

I _____ with my friends.

⊙ **sandwich**

샌드위치: two pieces of bread with cheese, meat, vegetables,
cooked eggs between them

The girl is eating a _____.

⊙ **delicious**

맛있는: very pleasant to taste or smell

The food is _____.

1   Choose the correct word for the blanks.

> Tony _____ listening to music.
> Eric _____ taking a shower.

ⓐ is   ⓑ does   ⓒ can

2   Choose the wrong answer.

> *A:* What are you doing now?
> *B:* _____

ⓐ I am making lunch.

ⓑ I am reading a book.

ⓒ I like soccer very much.

3   Choose the correct words for the blank.

Kevin _____ sleeping now.

ⓐ not is   ⓑ is not   ⓒ do not

4   Choose the correct sentence for the picture.

ⓐ Mary is watching TV.

ⓑ Grag is playing the piano.

ⓒ Dad is drinking water.

5 Complete the answer for the question.

What is the girl doing now?

_____ ice cream.

[6~7] Read the passage and answer the questions.

Paul's dad is reading a book.
Suddenly there is a ⓐnoise from Paul's room.

Dad: Paul, what is this noise?
Paul: Oh, Dad, it's nothing.
Dad: What are you doing? Did you break anything?
Paul: No, no. I am just playing with a dog.

But Paul doesn't look happy. The dog broke a vase. It is running around his room now.

＊broke: break(깨다)의 과거형

6 What is ⓐnoise?

ⓐ 강아지가 짖는 소리   ⓑ Paul의 비명 소리   ⓒ 꽃병이 깨지는 소리

7 Check T for true, F for false.

• Paul's dog broke the vase.   ___ T   ___ F
• Paul's dad is playing with the dog.   ___ T   ___ F

UNIT 03 How Was Your Vacation?

Listen and repeat the dialog. T09

- How was your summer vacation?
- It was wonderful!
  I took a trip to Hawaii with my family.
- Good! What did you do there?
- I swam in the sea and enjoyed the sun.

Speak aloud. T10

1

weekend / not fun
was sick in bed

2

vacation / good
visited Paris

Listen and choose the correct picture. T11

1 ⓐ    ⓑ    ⓒ

2 ⓐ    ⓑ    ⓒ

Listen and choose the correct answer. T11

1

   ⓑ   ⓒ

2

   ⓑ   ⓒ

37

Listen and repeat the words. T12

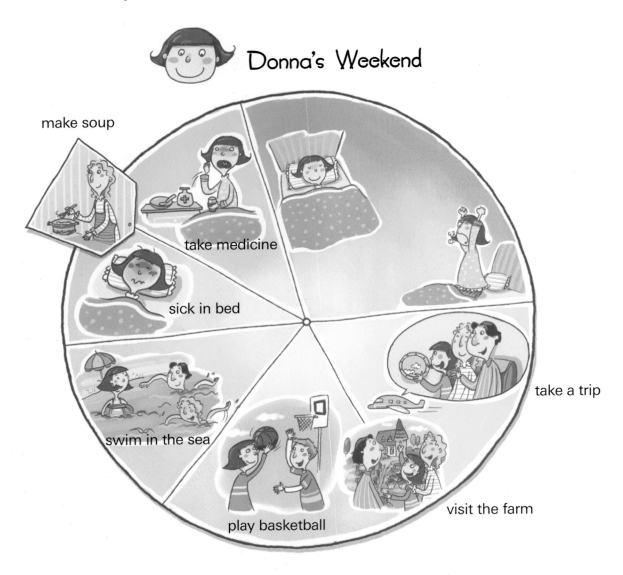

Donna's Weekend

make soup

take medicine

sick in bed

swim in the sea

play basketball

take a trip

visit the farm

Listen and choose the correct picture. T13

1 ⓐ

Thur.	Fri.	Sat.	Sun.
4	5	6	7
11	12	13	14
18	19	20	21
25	26	27	28

ⓑ

Mon.	Tues.	Wed.	Thur.
1	2	3	4
8	9	10	11
15	16	17	18
22	23	24	25

2 ⓐ   ⓑ

Circle the correct words for the picture.

1

take a trip

sick in bed

2

take medicine

play basketball

3

take a shower

swim in the sea

4

visit the farm

make soup

Unscramble the letters.

1

I make (p)(o)(s)(u).

_____

2

I take (m)(c)(e)(i)(d)(i)(n)(e).

_____

Choose the correct answer for the picture.

Q: What did you do yesterday?

1

    ⓐ I took a trip.

    ⓑ I made soup.

    ⓒ I was sick in bed.

2

    ⓐ I enjoyed the sun.

    ⓑ I swam in the sea.

    ⓒ I played basketball.

3

    ⓐ I had a cold and took medicine.

    ⓑ I went out to eat Chinese food.

    ⓒ I was sick but played baseball.

Choose and write the correct sentences to make a dialog.

 How was your trip to Paris?

 _____

 _____

 I visited the Eiffel Tower.

    ⓐ I took a trip to Paris.   ⓑ It was great. I had a good time.

    ⓒ What did you do there?   ⓓ What do you want to do there?

 **CHALLENGE!**

Choose the correct sentence for the blank.

1 *A:* How was your birthday party?

   B: _____

   Mom made a cake for me.

   ⓐ It was great.

   ⓑ It was pretty.

   ⓒ It was not fun.

2 *A:* What did you do yesterday?

   B: _____

   ⓐ I'm reading some comic books.

   ⓑ It was great. I had a good time there.

   ⓒ I helped my mom and made soup with her.

Read the dialog and answer the questions.

Eric: How was your weekend?

Lisa: It was good. I visited the farm with my family. _____ⓐ_____

Eric: It was terrible. I had a cold.

Lisa: That's too bad. Are you OK now?

Eric: Yes. I took medicine and took a rest.

1 Write the best expression in _____ⓐ_____ .

2 Which of the following is true?

   ⓐ Lisa was sick. She had a cold.

   ⓑ Eric's weekend was not good.

   ⓒ Eric went to the farm with his family.

Choose and write the correct sentences to complete the dialog.

I had a cold and took medicine.   I played basketball with my friends.

How was your holiday?   What did you do yesterday?

Yes, I had a great time.   No, it was not fun.

What did they do yesterday? Write sentences using the given words.

1

play soccer

_____

2

have a cold and take medicine

_____

Unscramble and write the sentence.

1 | made | . | soup | I |

_____

2 | fun | . | was | not | it |

_____

3 | was | ? | holiday | your | how |

_____

4 | yesterday | do | what | did | you | ? |

_____

Number the sentences in order and write them.

_____ It was great. I had a good time in Torino, Italy.

_____ What did you do there?

__1__ How was your winter vacation?

_____ I went skiing with my family.

1 How was your winter vacation? _____

2 _____

3 _____

4 _____

Summer Vacation

Complete the cartoon. If necessary, change the form.

This summer vacation, my family _____ my grandparents in Jeju.

My brother and I _____.

Suddenly it started raining.

We _____ in the rain.

| make soup | swim in the sea | visit |
| take medicine | play basketball | have |

That night, we _____ a cold. We were sick in bed.

My grandparents _____ for us.

We had the soup and _____.

Next morning, we got well and had a good time.

[1~3] Listen and choose the correct picture. ○ T14

1 ⓐ  ⓑ  ⓒ

2 ⓐ  ⓑ  ⓒ

3 ⓐ  ⓑ  ⓒ

[4~5] Listen and choose the correct answer. ○ T14

4   ⓑ ⓒ

5 ⓐ   ⓑ ⓒ

6 Choose the correct word for the blanks.

> I _____ a trip.
> I _____ medicine.
> I _____ a shower.

ⓐ play   ⓑ take   ⓒ have

[7~8] Read the dialog and answer the questions.

> *Julia*: How was your weekend?
>
> *Scott*: It was great.
>
>   I visited my grandparents.
>
>   _____ⓐ_____
>
> *Julia*: It was not good. I was sick in bed.

7 Which of the following is the best expression in _____ⓐ_____?

   ⓐ How was your weekend?

   ⓑ What are you doing?

   ⓒ What did you do there?

8 Which of the following is NOT true?

   ⓐ Scott visited his grandparents.

   ⓑ Julia and Scott talked about their vacation.

   ⓒ Julia didn't have a good time on her weekend.

UNIT 04 I Went to the Cinema

Quiz

Q: What did the girl do yesterday?

A: She _____ to the cinema and _____ a picture with a famous movie star.

Quiz

Q: How was Billy's weekend?

A: It was _____.

He had a _____ and was _____ in bed.

■ Question Words: How / What

How	'어떻게'라는 뜻으로 신체적, 정서적 건강상태를 물을 때나 어떤 일을 한 방법을 물을 때 사용한다. How are you? — I'm fine. How was your weekend? — It was terrible. How can I get to City Hall? — You can take the subway.
What	'무엇'이라는 뜻으로 사물이나 동작에 대해 물을 때 사용한다. What is this? — It's a bag. What are you doing? — I'm watering the plants. What did you do yesterday? — I went to the cinema.

Write a correct question word.

1 A: _____ is your mother?   B: She's fine.

2 A: _____ are they?   B: They are cows.

3 A: _____ is it?   B: It's an apple.

4 A: _____ was your vacation?   B: It was great.

5 A: _____ are you today?   B: I'm not so good.

6 A: _____ did you do yesterday?   B: I visited my grandparents.

7 A: _____ is Tom doing?   B: He is playing computer games.

8 A: _____ can I get to the cinema?   B: You can take the bus number 10.

Match pairs to make dialogs.

1 | How was your trip? | | I'm listening to music.

2 | What did you do last weekend? | | It was fantastic.

3 | What are you doing? | | I took the subway.

4 | How did you get to the library? | | I took a trip to Tokyo.

Unscramble the words to complete the dialog.

1   your   ?   how   holiday   was

A: _____

B: It was wonderful.

2   you   weekend   did   last   ?   do   what

A: _____

B: I went to the zoo with my friends.

3   England   a   took   trip   to   I

A: What did you do during your vacation?
B: _____ with my family.

■ Past Simple of Verbs

1. Regular verbs

Rules	Cases	Examples
add -ed	most verbs	visit → visited cook → cooked
add -d	verbs ending in -e	like → liked love → loved
drop -y and add -ied	verbs ending in 'a consonant + -y'	cry → cried study → studied
double the last consonant and add -ed	one-syllabled verbs ending in 'a vowel + a consonant'	stop → stopped step → stepped

2. Irregular verbs

Present	Past	Present	Past	Present	Past
am (is)	was	go	went	run	ran
are	were	see	saw	give	gave
do	did	take	took	come	came
have	had	make	made	put	put
say	said	swim	swam	cut	cut

Choose the correct word.

1 Last Saturday Jenny (visited / visites) her cousin Eric.
She (studies / studied) English with him.

2 Emma (is / was) very sick yesterday and she (goes / went) to bed early.

3 Jason (liked / likeed) hamburgers so much and he (haved / had) a hamburger every day.

Complete the sentences with the past form of the given verbs.

| play | make | go | take | visit |

1 John _____ his cousins in America.

2 Tommy _____ computer games all day.

3 Ann _____ to a museum with her sister.

4 Patty _____ soup for her mom yesterday.

5 Charlie _____ a trip to China during his holiday.

Complete the sentences with the given information.

What Dave Did Last Week

Monday	Tuesday	Wednesday	Thursday	Friday
swim in the sea	cut off branches	see a movie	run a marathon	do math homework

1 Dave _____ last Monday.

2 Dave _____ last Tuesday.

3 Dave _____ last Wednesday.

4 Dave _____ last Thursday.

5 Dave _____ last Friday.

The Lion and the Mouse  T15

One afternoon, a lion said, "I'm going to take a nap. You animals must be quiet."

A few minutes later, a little mouse went beside the lion.

She walked on tiptoes, but ⓐmake some noise.

The lion woke and said, "Snack time!"

"Please don't eat me. Some day I can help you," cried the little mouse.

"No kidding! You are so _____ⓑ_____! How can you help me?" the lion laughed at the little mouse and let her go.

---

1 밑줄 친 ⓐ의 알맞은 형태를 고르세요.

① makes   ② maked   ③ made

2 빈칸 ⓑ에 들어갈 알맞은 말을 고르세요.

① big   ② small   ③ fast

3 다음 중 윗글의 내용과 일치하지 않는 것을 고르세요.

① 사자는 잠시 낮잠을 자고 있었다.

② 사자가 자는 동안 쥐가 사자 옆으로 왔다.

③ 사자는 쥐를 용서하지 않았다.

The next day, two hunters came to the forest _____ⓒ_____ the lion.

They set a huge net.

The lion stepped into the net.

He cried and cried.

The little mouse heard him and

ran to help him.

"Don't move. I will chew the net,"

said the little mouse.

She cut the net with her teeth,

and the lion was free.

The lion thanked the little mouse

and said, "I learned a lesson today.

_____ⓓ_____ "

4 빈칸 ⓒ에 들어갈 알맞은 말을 고르세요.

① to help   ② to catch   ③ to play

5 빈칸 ⓓ에 들어갈 알맞은 말을 고르세요.

① Animals can not be friends.

② You should not help the lion.

③ Little friends can become great friends.

6 다음 중 윗글의 내용과 일치하지 않는 것을 고르세요.

① 사자는 도망간 쥐를 잡기 위해 그물을 쳤다.

② 쥐가 그물을 잘라 사자를 구해 주었다.

③ 사자는 그물을 잘라준 쥐에게 고맙다는 인사를 하였다.

Build up your word power.

⊙ nap

낮잠: a short sleep

I'm going to take a _____.

⊙ beside

··· 옆에, ··· 가까이에: at the side of, next to

A little mouse went _____ the lion.

⊙ tiptoes

발끝: the tips of the toes

She walked on _____.

⊙ wake 〔과거형: woke〕

잠이 깨다: to stop sleeping

The lion _____.

⊙ laugh 〔과거형: laughed〕

··· 을 비웃다: to make fun of somebody or something

The lion _____ at the little mouse.

⊙ hunter

사냥꾼: a person who hunts wild animals

The _____ came to the forest to catch the lion.

⊙ forest

숲: a large area of land covered with trees

Two hunters came to the _____.

⊙ huge

거대한: very large

They set a _____ net.

⊙ step 〔과거형: stepped〕

한 걸음을 내딛다: to raise one foot and put it down to walk
or move

The lion _____ into the net.

⊙ chew

…을 씹다, 깨물다: to use the teeth to break up

I will _____ the net.

⊙ thank 〔과거형: thanked〕

…에게 감사하다: to tell someone that you are grateful
for something

The lion _____ the little mouse.

⊙ learn 〔과거형: learned〕

배우다: to gain knowledge of a subject or skill through
education or experience

I _____ a lesson today.

1 Choose the correct word for the blanks.

> What _____ he do yesterday?
> What _____ you do last night?

ⓐ do   ⓑ did   ⓒ does

[2~3] Choose the correct sentence for the blank.

2

> A: _____
> B: It was not fun.

ⓐ How did you go there?

ⓑ How was your holiday?

ⓒ What did you do yesterday?

3

> A: _____
> B: I watched a show on TV.

ⓐ How was your weekend?

ⓑ What did you do last night?

ⓒ Where did you go during your holiday?

4 Choose the wrong part of the sentence.

I taked lots of pictures in London.
  ⓐ   ⓑ   ⓒ

5 Choose the correct sentence.

> *Kevin's diary*
>
> *Sunday, May 16th*
>
> I went hiking with my family yesterday. I played in the water. My parents cooked lunch. Suddenly, it started to rain. Today, I had a fever and I was sick in bed. It was a terrible holiday.

ⓐ Kevin had a wonderful weekend.

ⓑ Kevin cooked lunch with his father.

ⓒ Kevin went hiking with his family on Saturday.

[6~7] **Read the dialog and answer the questions.**

> *Brad:* How was your vacation?
> *Sue:* Oh, it was great. I went to China with my family.
>   I visited beautiful palaces and the Great Wall.
> *Brad:* Wow! Sounds fantastic! I'd like to go to China someday.
> *Sue:* How was yours, Brad?
> *Brad:* It was _____. I played soccer with friends and
>   got hurt. I was in hospital during the vacation.
> *Sue:* Oh, I am very sorry to hear that.

6 Which of the following is the most suitable for the blank?

ⓐ not fun   ⓑ not bad   ⓒ not long

7 Where did Sue go during her vacation?

ⓐ    ⓑ    ⓒ

Roller
coaster

Roller Coaster F1
Student Book

UNIT 01

P. 13

1 🎧 I'm listening to music. Who am I?

ⓐ

2 🎧 Jake is watering the plants. Who is Jake?

ⓒ

1 🎧 ⓐ I am a student.
ⓑ I like playing soccer.
ⓒ I am working on the computer.

ⓒ

2 🎧 ⓐ What do you do?
ⓑ What is your sister doing?
ⓒ Where are you?

ⓑ

🎧 ⓐ A: Where are you?
B: I am on the balcony.
ⓑ A: What are you doing?
B: I like English.
ⓒ A: What are you doing?
B: I am in my room.

ⓐ

P. 14

1 🎧 water the plants

ⓐ

2 🎧 wait for the bus

ⓑ

P. 15

make dinner

work on the computer

take a shower

wait for the bus

water the plants

listen to music

1 Mike is waiting for the bus.
2 His sister is watering the plants.
3 His dad is making dinner.
4 His mom is working on the computer.

P. 16

1 ⓐ   2 ⓑ   3 ⓒ   4 ⓒ

What are you doing?   I'm on the balcony.
Where are you?   I'm making a kite.

P. 17

1 ⓑ   2 ⓑ

Julie is making a cake and Kelly will help Julie.

P. 18

A boy is taking a shower.

A woman is making dinner.

A girl is reading a book.

A man is watering the plants.

1 A: What is she doing?
B: She is working on the computer.

2 A: What is the girl doing?
B: She is playing the piano.

P. 19

1 My brother is reading a book.
2 What is Ann doing now?
3 My father is on the balcony.
4 Mr. Baker is watering the flowers.

My family had dinner and now we are having a rest.
My mother is reading a book and my father is watering the plants.
My sister is listening to music.
Me? I am writing about my family.

P. 20~21

Mom, mom! Help me. I am making a kite.
Sorry, Fiona. I am busy. I am making dinner.
Sorry, Fiona. I am busy, too. I am watering the plants
Ask Sam.

What are you doing?
I am reading a book.
We are reading books.

P. 22~23

> 1 A woman is working on the computer.
> 2 A man is reading a book.
> 3 A girl is making a cake.
> 4 A boy is watering the flowers.

5
> A: Where is Ann?
> B: She is on the balcony.

ⓒ

6
> A: What is Ted doing now?
> B: He is listening to music.

ⓐ

7 ⓒ   8 ⓑ
9 ⓒ

/ 해석 / A: 주디, 엄마가 저녁 식사 준비하고 있는데. 도와 줄래.
        B: 알았어요, 엄마, 그런데 잠시만 기다려 주세요.
        A: 왜? 지금 뭐하는데?
        B: 샤워 중이에요.

10 ⓑ
/ 해석 / 샘: 안녕하세요, 윌슨 아줌마.
        윌슨 부인: 안녕, 샘.
        샘: 토니를 만나고 싶은데요. 집에 있어요?
        윌슨 부인: 토니는 지금 집에 없는데.
        샘: 그는 어디에 있어요?
        윌슨 부인: 토니는 도서관에 있어.

UNIT 02

P. 24~25

Q: It is 4 o'clock. What is Alice doing now?
A: She is eating now.

Q: Why is Alice crying?
A: Because of Ted's shirt.

P. 26

1 crying   2 going   3 walking
4 taking   5 making   6 hiking
7 running   8 cutting   9 shopping

1 They are cuting tomatoes.
2 Ann is going to the supermarket.
3 Mike and Jill are making pizza.
4 David's dog Benji is running after him.

P. 27

1 Ann is listening to music.
2 My brother is swimming in the pool.
3 I am eating a hamburger.
4 Paul and Cindy are making pizza.

Mr. Hudson is watching TV.
Ms. Hudson is reading a book.
Tim and Jake are making a kite together.
Miranda is cutting the paper. She wants to make a mask.

P. 28

1 A: Is he playing the piano?
  B: No, he is not playing the piano.
      He is playing the violin.
2 A: Are they eating spaghetti?
  B: No, they are not eating spaghetti.
      They are eating pizza.

P. 29

1 Is Tony watching TV?
2 Are you going to school?
3 Are they eating hamburgers?

1 I am not doing my homework.
2 My sister, Miranda is not playing the piano.
3 Mom and Dad are not reading books.

1 Are you making lunch?
2 Mary is not listening to music.

P. 30 ~ 31

1 ③   2 running   3 ②
4 ①   5 ③   6 ②

/ 해석 / 우리 학교에 온 걸 환영해

나는 팅이야. 나는 베이징에 살아. 매일 아침 내 여동생 지아오와 걸어서 학교에 가. 이제 너희들에게 우리 학교를 소개할게.

여기가 내가 다니는 학교야. 학생들이 많고 우리는 모두 좋은 친구들이야. 봐! 남자 아이들은 축구를 하고 여자 아이들은 운동장을 달리고 있어. 나도 축구를 좋아해.

이 곳은 우리 교실이야. 친구들이 그림을 그리고 있고 리 선생님께서 그들을 도와주고 계셔. 모두 웃고 있고 행복해 보여.

이 곳은 음악실이야. 학생들이 노래를 부르고 선생님께서 피아노를 치셔. 화음이 훌륭하지.

이 곳은 학교 도서관이야. 우리는 많은 책과 좋은 컴퓨터가 있어. 많은 학생들이 책을 읽고 몇몇 학생들은 컴퓨터로 작업하고 있어.

이 곳이 학교 식당이야. 우리는 여기서 점심을 먹어.

몇몇 여자 아이들은 샌드위치를 먹고 있고 몇몇 남자 아이들은 우유를 마시고 있어. 음식들은 맛있어.

우리 학교가 마음에 드니? 나는 우리 학교가 좋아.

P. 32 ~ 33

Every morning I walk to school.
This is my sister Jiao.
My brother is a middle school student.
This is my classroom.
My friends draw a picture together.
They smile.

The students sing.
This is a school library.
Now we are in a school cafeteria.
I talk with my friends.
The girl is eating a sandwich.
The food is delicious.

P. 34 ~ 35

1 ⓐ   2 ⓒ   3 ⓑ   4 ⓐ

5 She is eating ice cream.

6 ⓒ

7 Paul's dog broke the vase.   ✓ T   __ F
  Paul's dad is playing with the dog.   __ T   ✓ F

/ 해석 / 폴의 아빠는 책을 읽고 계신다.
        갑자기 폴의 방에서 소음이 난다.

    아빠: 폴, 이 소리가 뭐니?
    폴: 어, 아빠, 아무 것도 아니예요.
    아빠: 뭐 하고 있니? 뭐라도 깼니?
    폴: 아니, 아니예요. 그냥 개랑 놀고 있어요.

    그러나 폴이 좋아 보이지 않는다. 개는 꽃병을 깼다.
    개는 지금 폴의 방을 뛰어 다니고 있다.

UNIT 03

P. 37

1

> 🎧 A: How was your weekend?
> B: It was good. I played basketball with my father.

ⓐ

2

> 🎧 A: How was your school picnic?
> B: It was not fun. It rained a lot.

ⓑ

1

> 🎧 A: _____
> B: It was great.
>
> ⓐ How are you?
> ⓑ How was your vacation?
> ⓒ How can I get to the stadium?

ⓑ

2

> 🎧 A: How was your trip?
> B: _____
>
> ⓐ I was sick all day.
> ⓑ I cleaned my room.
> ⓒ I had a great time in London.

ⓒ

P. 38

1

> 🎧 weekend

ⓐ

2

> 🎧 play basketball

ⓑ

P. 39

1 take a trip	2 play basketball
3 swim in the sea	4 visit the farm

1 soup	2 medicine

P. 40

1 ⓒ   2 ⓑ   3 ⓐ

🧑 How was your trip to Paris?

👧 ⓑ It was great. I had a good time.

🧑 ⓒ What did you do there?

👧 I visited the Eiffel Tower.

P. 41

1 ⓐ   2 ⓒ

1 How about you? / How was your weekend (yours)?
2 ⓑ

P. 42

1 They played soccer.
2 The girl had a cold and took medicine.

P. 43

1 I made soup.
2 It was not fun.
3 How was your holiday?
4 What did you do yesterday?

2 - 3 - 1 - 4

1 How was your winter vacation?
2 It was great. I had a good time in Torino, Italy.
3 What did you do there?
4 I went skiing with my family.

P. 44~45

This summer vacation, I visited my grandparents in Jeju.
I swam in the sea.
We played basketball in the rain.
That night, we had a cold.
My grandparents made soup for us.
We had the soup and took medicine.

P. 46~47

1 farm

ⓑ

2 swim in the sea

ⓒ

3 I was sick in bed.

ⓐ

4 Q: How was your trip?
   ⓐ I did my homework.
   ⓑ It was fun.
   ⓒ I took a trip last weekend.

ⓑ

5 Q: What did you do during your vacation?
   ⓐ How was your holiday?
   ⓑ It was not fun.
   ⓒ I visited my aunt in Japan.

ⓒ

6 ⓑ   7 ⓐ   8 ⓑ

UNIT 04

P. 48~49

Q: What did the girl do yesterday?
A: She went to the cinema and took a picture with a famous movie star.

Q: How was Billy's weekend?
A: It was terrible (bad, not good).
   He had a cold and was sick in bed.

P. 50

1 A: How is your mother?
   B: She's fine.
2 A: What are they?
   B: They are cows.
3 A: What is it?
   B: It's an apple.
4 A: How was your vacation?
   B: It was great.
5 A: How are you today?
   B: I'm not so good.
6 A: What did you do yesterday?
   B: I visited my grandparents.
7 A: What is Tom doing?
   B: He is playing computer games.
8 A: How can I get to the cinema?
   B: You can take the bus number 10.

P. 51

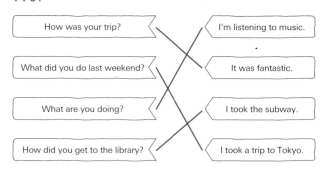

1 How was your holiday?
2 What did you do last weekend?
3 I took a trip to England with my family.

P. 52

1 Last Saturday Jenny visited her cousin Eric. She studied English with him.

2 Emma was very sick yesterday and she went to bed early.

3 Jason liked hamburgers so much and he had a hamburger every day.

P. 53

1 John visited his cousins in America.

2 Tommy played computer games all day.

3 Ann went to a museum with her sister.

4 Patty made soup for her mom yesterday.

5 Charlie took a trip to China during his holiday.

1 Dave swam in the sea last Monday.

2 Dave cut off branches last Tuesday.

3 Dave saw a movie last Wednesday.

4 Dave ran a marathon last Thursday.

5 Dave did math homework last Friday.

P. 54~55

| 1 ③ | 2 ② | 3 ③ |
| 4 ② | 5 ③ | 6 ① |

/ 해석 / 사자와 쥐

어느 날 오후, 사자가 "나는 낮잠을 좀 잘 것이다.
너희 동물들은 조용히 하거라."라고 말했다.
잠시 후, 작은 쥐 한 마리가 사자 옆으로 갔다.
쥐는 발끝으로 살금살금 걸었지만 소음이 났다.
사자가 깨어 말했다, "간식 시간이군!"
"제발 절 먹지 말아 주세요.
언젠가 제가 당신을 도울 수 있을 거예요."
작은 쥐가 울면서 말했다.
"농담하지 마라! 넌 너무 작아! 날 어떻게 도울 수 있겠니?"
사자는 작은 쥐를 비웃고는 가게 내버려 두었다.
다음 날, 사냥꾼 두 명이 사자를 잡으러 숲 속에 나타났다.
그들은 거대한 그물을 설치했다.
사자는 그물 안으로 발을 들여 놓고 말았다.
사자는 울고 또 울었다.
작은 쥐가 사자의 소리를 듣고 돕기 위해 달려갔다.
"움직이지 마세요. 제가 그물을 잘라 드릴게요." 작은 쥐가 말했다.

쥐는 이빨로 그물을 잘랐고 사자는 풀려났다.
사자는 작은 쥐에게 고마움을 표하며
"나는 오늘 작은 미물도 훌륭한 친구가 될 수 있다는 교훈을 얻었다."
라고 말했다.

P. 56~57

I'm going to take a nap.
A little mouse went beside the lion.
She walked on tiptoes.
The lion woke.
The lion laughed at the little mouse.
The hunter came to the forest to catch the lion.

Two hunters came to the forest.
They set a huge net.
The lion stepped into the net.
I will chew the net.
The lion thanked the little mouse.
I learned a lesson today.

P. 58~59

| 1 ⓑ | 2 ⓑ | 3 ⓑ | 4 ⓐ |
| 5 ⓒ | | | |

/ 해석 /　　　　　　케빈의 일기
　　　　　　　　　　　　　5월 16일 일요일

나는 어제 가족과 함께 하이킹을 갔다. 나는 물에 들어가 놀았다.
부모님께서 점심 식사를 준비하셨다. 갑자기 비가 내리기 시작했다.
오늘 나는 열이 나 아파서 누워 있었다. 아주 끔찍한 휴일이었다.

| 6 ⓐ | 7 ⓒ |

/ 해석 /　브래드: 방학은 어떻게 보냈니?
　　　수:　어, 좋았어. 가족이랑 중국에 갔었어.
　　　　　　멋진 궁전들이랑 만리장성을 방문했어.
　　　브래드: 왜! 정말 멋진데! 나도 중국에 가고 싶다.
　　　수:　너는 어떻게 보냈어, 브래드?
　　　브래드: 좋지 않았어. 친구들이랑 축구하다 다쳤어.
　　　　　　방학 동안 병원에 있었지.
　　　수:　어, 그거 안됐구나.

Roller Coaster
Workbook & Test

UNIT 01

P. 2

B

m	s	w	a	t	e	r	i	m
u	t	e	r	w	a	i	t	e
s	e	l	a	o	n	g	f	s
i	y	q	n	r	q	o	e	g
c	p	q	u	k	p	l	a	y
s	l	i	s	t	e	n	i	o
b	a	l	c	o	n	y	t	h
e	n	m	a	k	e	t	a	w
d	t	e	d	i	n	n	e	r

1	listen	2	water
3	plant	4	music
5	wait	6	balcony
7	make	8	work
9	dinner	10	play

P. 5

D

1 water the plants
2 take a shower
3 make dinner
4 wait for the bus
5 work on the computer
6 listen to music

E

Ⅰ ①Where is Sam?
  He is ②on the balcony.
Ⅱ ③What are you doing now?
  I'm ④making a cake.
Ⅲ My friends are ⑤in my room.

UNIT 02

P. 7

B

s	s	a	n	d	w	i	c	h
o	i	w	y	e	a	l	l	k
u	s	q	c	l	l	s	a	s
e	t	a	u	i	k	i	s	m
d	r	a	w	i	n	g	r	l
b	e	l	u	o	v	e	o	i
e	r	k	a	u	n	r	o	n
i	t	e	r	s	t	u	m	g
l	i	b	r	a	r	y	x	z

1	sandwich	2	library
3	sister	4	delicious
5	classroom	6	sing
7	talk	8	walk
9	drawing	10	smiling

P. 10

D

1	talking	2	drawing
3	eating	4	making
5	library	6	running

E

1 The baby is smiling happily.
2 Donna is cutting the paper.
3 Are they walking to the park?
4 He is not doing his homework.
5 Some students are drinking milk.
6 I am reading books in the library.

Workbook & Test

UNIT 03

P. 12

B

1 sick
2 weekend
3 vacation
4 medicine

C

1 take a trip
2 swim in the sea
3 visit the farm
4 make soup
5 play basketball

P. 15

E

1 take a trip
2 visit the farm
3 play basketball
4 swim in the sea
5 make soup
6 take medicine

F

I ①How was your holiday?
　It was ②wonderful.
II ③What did you do there?
　I ④swam in the sea and enjoyed the sun.
III ⑤How was yours?
　I was ⑥sick in bed yesterday.

UNIT 04

P. 17

B

1 forest
2 hunter
3 chew
4 tiptoe
5 cinema
6 take a nap

C

1 did
2 went
3 had
4 took
5 was
6 learned

7 swam
8 said
9 ran
10 cut
11 heard
12 woke
13 were
14 visited
15 saw
16 came

P. 20

E

1 cinema
2 terrible
3 chew
4 forest
5 take a nap
6 heard

F

1 How can I get to City Hall?
2 You can take the subway.
3 The hunter set a huge net.
4 She walked on tiptoes.
5 The lion laughed at the little mouse.
6 He took a picture with a famous movie star.

Achievement Test

1 ⓑ　　2 ⓐ　　3 ⓑ　　4 ⓒ
5 ⓐ　　6 ⓒ　　7 ⓑ　　8 ⓑ
9 ⓐ　　10 ⓒ

11 Are they drawing pictures?
12 Rebecca is not studying English.

Final Test

1 ⓒ　　2 ⓐ　　3 ⓑ　　4 ⓑ
5 ⓒ　　6 ⓐ　　7 ⓒ　　8 ⓒ
9 ⓐ　　10 ⓑ　　11 ⓒ　　12 ⓑ

01 I'm Watering the Plants

 Write and say aloud.

1	발코니	balcony
2	맛있는	delicious
3	도서관	library
4	저녁 식사를 준비하다	make dinner
5	농구를 하다	play basketball
6	음악을 듣다	listen to music
7	화초에 물을 주다	water the plants
8	버스를 기다리다	wait for the bus
9	책을 읽다	read a book
10	피아노 치다	play the piano
11	컴퓨터로 작업하다	work on the computer
12	샤워하다	take a shower

m	s	w	a	t	e	r	i	m
u	t	e	r	w	a	i	t	e
s	e	l	a	o	n	g	f	s
i	y	q	n	r	q	o	e	g
c	p	q	u	k	p	l	a	y
s	l	i	s	t	e	n	i	o
b	a	l	c	o	n	y	t	h
e	n	m	a	k	e	t	a	w
d	t	e	d	i	n	n	e	r

1 듣다 _____

2 물을 주다 _____

3 식물 _____

4 음악 _____

5 기다리다 _____

6 발코니 _____

7 만들다 _____

8 일하다 _____

9 저녁 식사 _____

10 놀다 _____

C Write and say aloud.

1 너는 어디에 있니?

Where are you?

2 나는 부엌에 있어.

I am in the kitchen.

3 Jack은 무엇을 하고 있니?

What is Jack doing?

4 그는 화분에 물을 주고 있어.

He is watering the plants.

5 나는 저녁 식사를 준비하고 있어.

I am making dinner.

6 너의 부모님은 어디 계시니?

Where are your parents?

7 나는 도서관에 있어.

I am in the library.

8 Sam은 무엇을 하고 있니?

What is Sam doing?

9 나는 꽃에 물을 주고 있어.

I am watering the flowers.

10 나는 점심 식사를 준비하고 있어.

I am making lunch.

D Listen and write the word. 🎧 💿 T16

1 _____

2 _____

3 _____

4 _____

5 _____

6 _____

E Listen and fill in the blanks. 🎧 💿 T16

I ① _____ is Sam?

He is ② _____ .

II ③ _____ are you _____ now?

I'm ④ _____ .

III My friends are ⑤ _____ .

02 What Is Alice Doing?

A Write and say aloud.

1	걷다	walk
2	걷고 있는	walking
3	만들다	make
4	만들고 있는	making
5	학생	student
6	교실	classroom
7	그리다	draw
8	그리고 있는	drawing
9	웃다	smile
10	웃고 있는	smiling
11	수영하다	swim
12	수영하고 있는	swimming
13	도서관	library
14	식당	cafeteria
15	말하다	talk
16	말하고 있는	talking
17	샌드위치	sandwich
18	맛있는	delicious

B Circle and write the word.

s	s	a	n	d	w	i	c	h
o	i	w	y	e	a	l	l	k
u	s	q	c	l	l	s	a	s
e	t	a	u	i	k	i	s	m
t	e	t	h	c	t	n	s	i
d	r	a	w	i	n	g	r	l
b	e	l	u	o	v	e	o	i
e	r	k	a	u	n	r	o	n
i	t	e	r	s	t	u	m	g
l	i	b	r	a	r	y	x	z

1 샌드위치 _____

2 도서관 _____

3 언니, 여동생 _____

4 맛있는 _____

5 교실 _____

6 노래하다 _____

7 말하다 _____

8 걷다 _____

9 그리고 있는 _____

10 웃고 있는 _____

C Write and say aloud.

1 소년은 울고 있다.

The boy is crying.

(부정문) The boy is not crying.

(의문문) Is the boy crying?

2 그들은 자고 있다.

They are sleeping.

(부정문) _____

(의문문) _____

3 너의 오빠는 TV를 보고 있다.

Your brother is watching TV.

(부정문) _____

(의문문) _____

4 너의 친구들은 햄버거를 먹고 있다.

Your friends are eating hamburgers.

(부정문) _____

(의문문) _____

5 소녀는 울고 있다.

The girl is crying.

(부정문) _____

(의문문) _____

6 아이들이 자고 있다.

The children are sleeping.

(부정문) _____

(의문문) _____

7 너의 여동생은 TV를 보고 있다.

Your sister is watching TV.

(부정문) _____

(의문문) _____

8 내 친구들은 샌드위치를 먹고 있다.

My friends are eating sandwiches.

(부정문) _____

(의문문) _____

D Listen and write the word. T17

1 _____

2 _____

3 _____

4 _____

5 _____

6 _____

E Listen and fill in the blanks. T17

1 The baby is _____ happily.

2 Donna is _____ the paper.

3 Are they _____ to the _____?

4 He is _____ _____ his homework.

5 Some _____ are _____ milk.

6 I am _____ books in the _____.

03 How Was Your Vacation?

A Write and say aloud.

1	방학	vacation
2	휴일	holiday
3	멋진	wonderful
4	주말	weekend
5	여행하다	take a trip
6	농구하다	play basketball
7	바다에서 수영하다	swim in the sea
8	아파서 누워 있다	sick in bed
9	학교 소풍	school picnic
10	약을 먹다	take medicine
11	농장을 방문하다	visit the farm
12	스프를 만들다	make soup

B Unscramble and write the word.

1 아픈 (c)(i)(k)(s) _____

2 주말 (e)(k)(e)(d)(n)(e)(w) _____

3 방학 (v)(a)(c)(i)(o)(n)(t)(a) _____

4 약 (m)(i)(e)(c)(n)(i)(d)(e) _____

C Fill in the blank and write the words.

make	basketball	farm	take	swim

1 _____ a trip _____

2 _____ in the sea _____

3 visit the _____ _____

4 _____ soup _____

5 play _____ _____

12

D Write and say aloud.

1 너는 방학을 어떻게 보냈니?

How was your vacation?

2 가족과 함께 하와이로 여행을 다녀 왔어.

I took a trip to Hawaii with my family.

3 나는 어제 아파서 누워 있었어.

I was sick in bed yesterday.

4 어제는 무엇을 했니?

What did you do yesterday?

5 그들은 농구를 했어.

They played basketball.

6 너는 휴일을 어떻게 보냈니?

How was your holiday?

_____

7 부모님과 함께 파리로 여행을 다녀 왔어.

I took a trip to Paris with my parents.

_____

8 나는 지난 주말에 아파서 누워 있었어.

I was sick in bed last weekend.

_____

9 거기서 무엇을 했어?

What did you do there?

_____

10 아이들은 축구를 했어.

The children played soccer.

_____

E Listen and write the word. 🎧 💿 T18

1 _____

2 _____

3 _____

4 _____

5 _____

6 _____

F Listen and fill in the blanks. 🎧 💿 T18

Ⅰ ① _____ was your _____?

It was ② _____.

Ⅱ ③ _____ did you do _____?

I ④ _____ and enjoyed the sun.

Ⅲ ⑤ _____ was _____?

I was ⑥ _____ yesterday.

15

04 I Went to the Cinema

A Write and say aloud.

1	극장	cinema
2	(잠에서) 깨다	wake
3	(잠에서) 깼다	woke
4	사진을 찍다	take a picture
5	사진을 찍었다	took a picture
6	(껌 등을) 씹다	chew
7	낮잠 자다	take a nap
8	발끝	tiptoe
9	소음을 내다	make noise
10	소음을 냈다	made noise
11	…을 비웃다	laugh at
12	…을 비웃었다	laughed at
13	사냥꾼	hunter
14	숲	forest
15	끔찍한	terrible

B Write the word.

1 숲 _____

2 사냥꾼 _____

3 씹다 _____

4 발끝 _____

5 극장 _____

6 낮잠 자다 _____

C Write the past simple form of each verb.

1 do – _____

2 go – _____

3 have – _____

4 take – _____

5 am/is – _____

6 learn – _____

7 swim – _____

8 say – _____

9 run – _____

10 cut – _____

11 hear – _____

12 wake – _____

13 are – _____

14 visit – _____

15 see – _____

16 come – _____

D Write and say aloud.

1 나는 방으로 달려 들어갔다.

I ran into the room.

2 소녀는 소란을 피웠다.

The girl made noise.

3 작은 쥐 한 마리가 사자 옆으로 갔다.

A little mouse went beside the lion.

4 나는 어제 약을 먹었다.

I took medicine yesterday.

5 우리 가족은 영화를 봤다.

My family watched a movie.

6 나는 화장실로 달려 들어갔다.

I ran into the bathroom.

7 소년은 소란을 피웠다.

The boy made noise.

8 Ann은 그녀의 강아지 옆으로 갔다.

Ann went beside her puppy.

9 내 남동생은 어제 약을 먹었다.

My brother took medicine yesterday.

10 내 친구와 나는 영화를 봤다.

My friend and I watched a movie.

E Listen and write the word. 🎧 💿 T19

1 _____

2 _____

3 _____

4 _____

5 _____

6 _____

F Listen and fill in the blanks. 🎧 💿 T19

1 _____ can I _____ to City Hall?

2 You can _____ the _____.

3 The _____ set a _____ net.

4 She _____ on _____.

5 The lion _____ the little _____.

6 He _____ with a _____ movie star.

Roller
Coaster

A Successful Start to Study English

[1-2] Choose the correct picture for the words.

1. water the plants

ⓐ    ⓑ   ⓒ

2. take a shower

ⓐ    ⓑ   ⓒ

[3-4] Choose the correct sentence for the picture.

3.

ⓐ The girl is making dinner.
ⓑ The girl is reading a book.
ⓒ The girl is playing the piano.

4.

ⓐ The boy is listening to music.
ⓑ The boy is waiting for the bus.
ⓒ The boy is working on the computer.

[5-6] Choose the correct sentence for the blank.

5.
| A: _____ |
| B: I am on the balcony. |

ⓐ Where are you?
ⓑ How are you today?
ⓒ What are you doing?

6.
| A: What are you doing now? |
| B: _____ |

ⓐ Yes, I am.
ⓑ He is in his room.
ⓒ I am making a kite.

[7-8] **Choose the wrong part of the sentence.**

7. My friend, Sam and I are swim in the pool.
              ⓐ   ⓑ   ⓒ

8. My family is eating dinner together.
           ⓐ   ⓑ   ⓒ

[9-10] **Read and answer the questions.**

> I am in the park near my house. A man and his dog are running together.
> A baby is falling down on the ground and _____. Her mom is helping her.
> Some boys are playing basketball.
> What am I doing? I am sitting on the beach and watching them.

9. Which of the following is best for the blank?

   ⓐ crying   ⓑ smiling   ⓒ eating

10. Which of the following is NOT true?

    ⓐ I am in the park.
    ⓑ A little girl is falling down.
    ⓒ I am playing soccer with my friends.

11. **Write a question sentence.**

    They are drawing pictures.

    _____

12. **Write a negative sentence.**

    Rebecca is studying English.

    _____

8.

A: What are you doing?
B: _____

ⓐ I took a shower.
ⓑ I am in my room.
ⓒ I am watering the flowers.

9. **Choose the wrong part of the sentence.**

David <u>runed</u> a <u>marathon</u> last <u>weekend</u>.
     ⓐ   ⓑ   ⓒ

10. **Choose the correct word for the blanks.**

_____ was your trip?
_____ is your mother?
_____ can I go to City Hall?

ⓐ Who   ⓑ How   ⓒ What

[11-12] **Read and answer the questions.**

Baby Mouse had the hiccups.

"Did you have some water?" asked Mama Mouse.

"Yes, but it didn't work. Hic! Hic!"

That moment Cricket appeared and said, "I can help you!"

Cricket came to Baby Mouse and she spoke in his ear.

"Eek!" Baby Mouse jumped off his bed. And Baby Mouse stopped his hiccups.

"What did you say?" asked Papa Mouse.

Cricket smiled and said, "Meow!"

*hiccup: 딸꾹질 *appear: 나타나다

11. Who helped Baby Mouse?

ⓐ Mama Mouse   ⓑ Papa Mouse   ⓒ Cricket

12. Which of the following is NOT true?

ⓐ Baby Mouse drank water.
ⓑ Mouse family had the hiccups.
ⓒ Water didn't work for the hiccups.

Final Test

Name 　　　　　　**Score**

[1-3] Choose the correct picture for the words.

1. hunter

 ⓐ　 ⓑ　 ⓒ

2. take medicine

 ⓐ　 ⓑ　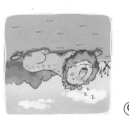 ⓒ

3. visit the farm

 ⓐ　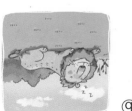 ⓑ　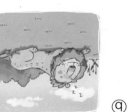 ⓒ

[4-5] Choose the correct sentence for the picture.

4.

ⓐ The girl took a shower.
ⓑ The girl was sick in bed.
ⓒ The girl swam in the sea.

5.

ⓐ The lion cried and cried.
ⓑ The lion walked on tiptoes.
ⓒ The lion stepped into the net.

[6-8] Choose the correct sentence for the blank.

6. A: How was your holiday?
   B: _____

ⓐ It was wonderful.
ⓑ I'm reading a book.
ⓒ I was on the balcony.

7. A: _____
   B: I played soccer with my friends.

ⓐ What are you doing?
ⓑ How did you go to school?
ⓒ What did you do yesterday?